Jewish Migration

John Bliss

Raintree

Chicago, Illinois

© 2012 Raintree
an imprint of Capstone Global Library, LLC
Chicago, Illinois

Edited by Louise Galpine, Abby Colich, and Diyan Leake
Designed by Richard Parker
Original illustrations © Capstone Global Library Ltd 2011
Illustrated by Jeff Edwards
Picture research by Mica Brancic

Originated by Capstone Global Library Ltd
Printed and bound in China by CTPS

15 14 13 12 11
10 9 8 7 6 5 4 3 2 1

Library of Congress Cataloging-in-Publication Data
Bliss, John, 1958-
  Jewish migration / John Bliss.—ed. 1
    p. cm.—(Children's true stories: migration)
  Includes bibliographical references and index.
  ISBN 978-1-4109-4075-9 (hc)—ISBN 978-1-4109-4081-0 (pb) 1. Jews—Europe—Migrations—Juvenile literature. I. Title. II. Series.

  DS135.E83B55 2011   9767
  305.892'404—dc22   2010039334

Acknowledgments
We would like to thank the following for permission to reproduce photographs: The Art Archive p. **6** (Domenica del Corriere/Alfredo Dagli Orti); Bridgeman Art Library p. **13** (© SZ Photo); Getty Images pp. **11** (Popperfoto), **15** (Popperfoto), **16** (Hulton Archive/General Photographic Agency), **18** (Hulton Archive/Fred Morley), **20** (Hulton Archive/Fox Photos/Reg Speller), **23** (Brian Hendler); Illinois Holocaust Museum & Education Center p. **12** (Brill Family Resource Center); Ralph Rehbock p. **17**; Rex Features pp. **24** (Israel Sun/Y Tzur), **27** (Alex Segre); Shutterstock p. **26** (Protasov Alexey); University of Wisconsin-Milwaukee pp. **7**, **9**, **10**; Alona Naeil Yalda p. **25**.

Cover photograph of 500 Jewish refugees ranging from 7 to 17 years old, mainly from Vienna, Austria, gathered in Lowestoft, Suffolk, England, December 13, 1938, reproduced with permission of Corbis (© Austrian Archives).

We would like to acknowledge the following sources of material: pp. 7–11 from "Golda Meir," University of Wisconsin Digital Collections, http://digicoll.library.wisc.edu/cgi-bin/WI/WI-idx?type=HTML&rgn=DIV1&byte=237485895; pp. **12–17** from the Illinois Museum and Holocaust Center website, "Witness to the Holocaust: Ralph Rehbock," http://www.ilholocaustmuseum.org/pages/witness_archive/145.php?id=1/. Accessed on November 19, 2010; pp. **19–21** from "Vienna, 1938: A Child's View" by Kurt Fuchel, http://www.kindertransport.org/voices/fuchel_vienna.htm. Accessed on November 19, 2010; pp. **22–25** from an email exchange with Alona Poupesheva, June 10–12, 2010.

We would like to thank Professor Sarah Chinn for her invaluable help in the preparation of this book.

Disclaimer

Contents

DAILY LIFE
Read here to learn what life was like for the children in these stories, and the impact that migrating had at home and at school.

NUMBER CRUNCHING
Find out the details about migration and the numbers of people involved.

Migrants' Lives
Read these boxes to find out what happened to the children in this book when they grew up.

HELPING HAND
Find out how people and organizations have helped children to migrate.

On the Scene
Read eyewitness accounts of migration in the migrants' own words.

Some words are printed in bold, **like this**. You can find out what they mean by looking in the glossary on page 30.

A Wandering People

Jewish people follow the religion of Judaism. The Jewish people originally came from the land that is now Israel. Today, Jewish people live all around the world.

Being Jewish has more to do with **culture** (a person's values and beliefs) than where they are from. Jews may be German, Russian, British, or many other nationalities.

Migration is part of Jewish history. The Bible tells of Jewish people wandering in the Sinai Desert 3,400 years ago. Jews have often suffered from **anti-Semitism**, which means **prejudice** against Jewish people. At times, people disagreed with the Jewish religion and blamed Jews for many troubles. In some countries, Jews were forced to live in **ghettos**, parts of the city away from everyone else.

A permanent home

After **World War II**, the modern state of Israel was created. Although many Jewish people migrated to Israel, many more continue to live in other countries.

NUMBER CRUNCHING

From the Middle East, Jewish people have spread to nations around the world. There are now more Jews living in the United States than in Israel. Today, Jewish people continue to flee anti-Semitism in countries such as Syria, Lebanon, and several African nations.

This painting shows a Jewish ghetto
in Italy in 1888.

Russia: 1901

In the 1800s and early 1900s, Jewish people in Russia were sometimes attacked in **pogroms**. A pogrom was organized violence against Jewish people by non-Jews. Often the police knew about pogroms and did nothing to stop them.

Russian pogroms often left Jews homeless and injured.

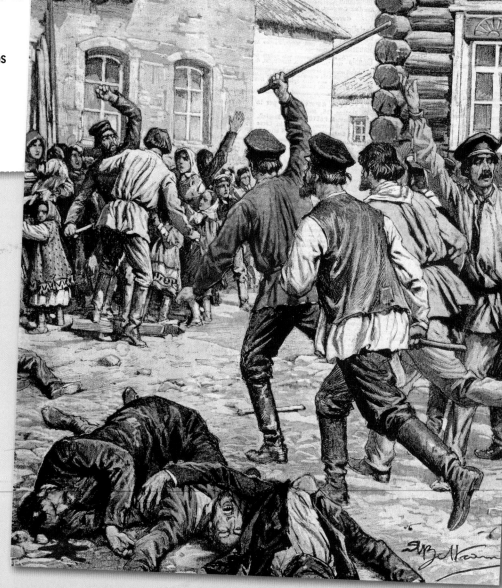

Golda Mabovitch

Golda Mabovitch was born in 1898 in Kiev, which was part of Russia at the time. Today, Kiev is the capital city of the Ukraine. Life in Kiev was difficult for the Mabovitch family. Jewish people were not allowed to own land, and the **government** decided where they could live. The family lived in fear of pogroms.

When Golda was five years old, her father, Moshe, decided to move the family to the United States. Moshe went first, to find work and save money to bring the rest of the family over. Meanwhile, Golda's mother moved with her three daughters to the city of Pinsk. Her family lived there, waiting for news from the United States.

In this picture, Golda Mabovitch is wearing traditional Russian dress.

DAILY LIFE

When Golda lived in Pinsk, nearly three-quarters of the population was Jewish. Many Jews owned businesses, but there were many laws to limit the rights of Jews. For example, only 10 percent of Jewish children could attend public schools.

The New World

Three years later, Moshe sent for his family. Golda, her mother, Blume, and her sisters, Sheyna and Tzipke, traveled by ship from Russia to the United States. It took two weeks. They then had to travel nearly 1,600 kilometers (1,000 miles) further, to Milwaukee, Wisconsin, in the middle of the country.

The distance from Kiev to Milwaukee is 8,050 kilometers (5,000 miles). The journey for Golda's family was even further because they traveled by land and sea.

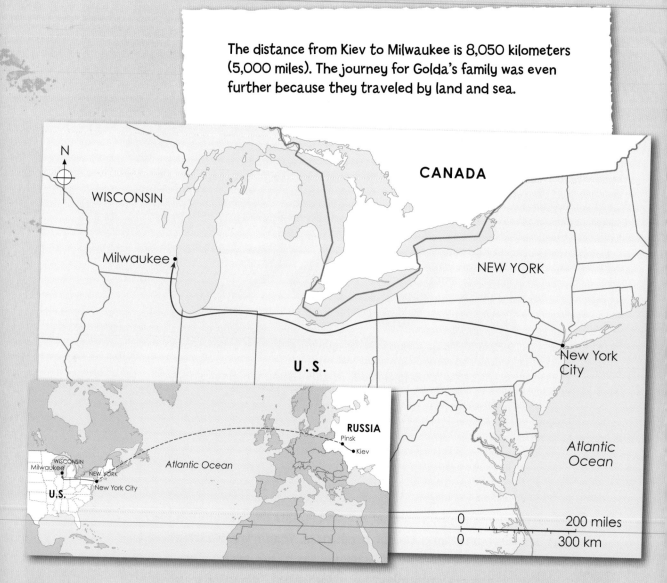

Many **immigrant** children found their life in the United States an adventure. Everything was new. Golda traveled in a car for the first time. She was amazed by all the traffic in the streets. In the city of Milwaukee, she went into the tallest building she had ever seen. It was five stories high.

Golda was 16 when this picture was taken. She is on the left.

DAILY LIFE

Moshe Mabovitch liked being an American, and he wanted the same for his daughters. On their first day in Milwaukee, he took them shopping for new clothes. Golda's older sister, Sheyna, refused to dress like an American. Golda, on the other hand, loved her new outfit.

Growing up

Golda's family lived in a small apartment in a poor Jewish neighborhood. Her mother took over an empty store in the building and opened a fruit and vegetable store. Like many children, Golda was expected to help in the store. This often made her late for school. When Golda complained, her mother just said, "We have to live, don't we?"

School was important to Golda. When she was about nine years old, she organized a group to raise money to buy schoolbooks for poor children. She called the group the American Young Sisters Society. Later, she said this was her "first public work." It would not be her last.

Many of Golda's classmates at the Fourth Street School were also immigrants from other lands.

Golda Meir

In 1921 Golda and her husband, Morris Myerson, moved to **Palestine**, as Israel was then called. She later shortened her last name to Meir. Golda worked with the organization that created the state of Israel after World War II, and she signed its Declaration of Independence in 1948. In 1969 she became the prime minister of Israel.

As the prime minister of Israel, Golda Meir was one of the most powerful women in the world.

Germany: 1938

In 1933 the National Socialist Party, led by Adolf Hitler, came to power in Germany. This group, also called the **Nazis**, blamed the Jewish people for many of Germany's problems. Within a few years, Jewish men, women, and children were sent to prisons called **concentration camps**. Millions were murdered. This period is called the **Holocaust**.

Ralph Rehbock

Ralph Rehbock was born in Germany in 1934. At that time, few people suspected how bad things would get for the Jewish people. Ralph had a happy childhood, with toys and games and plenty to eat. But soon the trouble started.

Ralph Rehbock was four years old when he and his parents escaped from the Nazis.

Jewish people lost many of their rights. Their children could no longer go to school. Ralph's mother lost her job, because Jews were not allowed to work for non-Jewish people. In 1938 the family decided to leave Germany. Ralph was four years old.

In one night, the German government arrested thousands of Jews. Jewish people were ordered to show a Star of David as a sign that they were different from other people.

On the scene

Ralph's parents protected him from the events around them. In Germany, he knew he had to step off the sidewalk when he passed Nazi soldiers, but he did not know this was because he was Jewish.

To Berlin!

Ralph's family traveled to Berlin, Germany's capital city, to get the papers they needed to leave the country. That evening Ralph's father received a phone call telling him that Nazi soldiers were looking for him.

Later that night, 30,000 Jews were arrested in Germany. Jewish homes and places of worship were destroyed. Luckily, Ralph's father was able to escape to the United Kingdom.

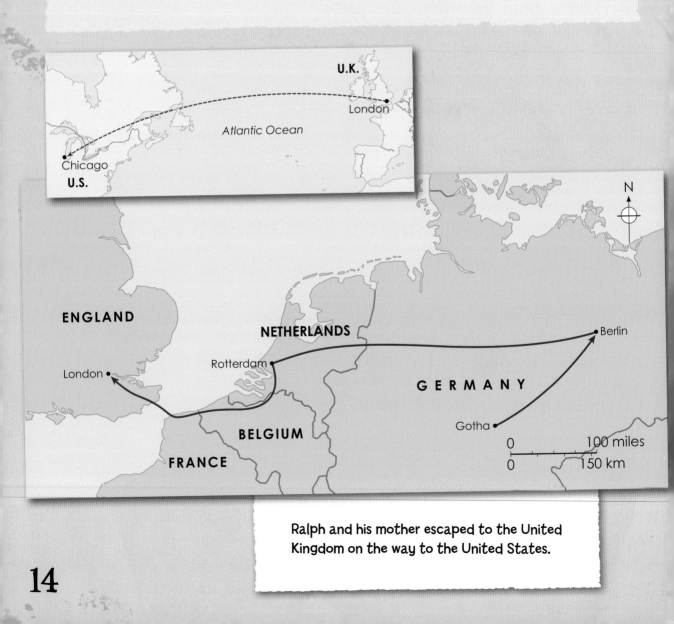

Ralph and his mother escaped to the United Kingdom on the way to the United States.

Out of Germany

Ralph and his mother left Berlin the next month. They boarded a train to take them out of the country. But when they reached the border with the Netherlands, all of the Jews had to leave the train.

As they were waiting at the station, a stranger came up to them. He told them to follow him. They ran across the railroad tracks and got onto a train going in a different direction. A few minutes later, the train was in the Netherlands. They were free!

A stranger helped Ralph and his mother escape from the Nazis at a station like this.

NUMBER CRUNCHING

More than one million Jewish children were killed by the Nazis. Thousands of other children, who had physical or mental illnesses, also died.

A new life

Ralph's mother had relatives who lived in Chicago, Illinois, in the United States. The Rehbocks moved there. They rented a small apartment on the south side of Chicago.

Ralph lived with his cousins for several months. The family had all been born in the United States and did not speak German. Ralph's parents wanted him to learn English. He also learned American **customs**. Ralph arrived in the United States in December. When he started school the following September, he spoke English well enough to fit in with the other children.

Ralph lived with his cousins in the Hyde Park neighborhood of Chicago. Parts of Chicago looked like this in the 1930s.

Ralph's parents never spoke German again. They were angry with the country that had treated them so badly. The family put the past behind them.

Today, Ralph tells his story to adults and children. It is his way of keeping history alive.

Ralph Rehbock

Today, Ralph Rehbock **volunteers** with the Illinois Holocaust Museum in Skokie, Illinois. As part of his work, he tells his story to young audiences. Ralph tells about the stranger who saved him and his mother, to remind people that even small acts of kindness can make a huge difference.

Austria: 1939

Not all the children who fled Germany left with their families. Some escaped through the **Kindertransport**. This was an organization that saved nearly 10,000 Jewish children from Germany and the surrounding countries.

For some children, the journey was an adventure. For others, it was scary.

Kurt Fuchel

Kurt Fuchel grew up in Vienna, Austria. His father was a bank manager, and his family lived well. When Hitler came to power, Kurt's father lost his job. Then a woman came to their apartment and said they had to leave. She was going to live there now. Kurt's family was just one of many who lost their homes in this way.

On the scene

Kurt Fuchel remembers his father telling him he was leaving home.

"One day Papa tells me that we are going to move again, but not together. He and Mutti [Mama] will put me on a train and some nice people will meet me in a place called England. . . . He says, 'This is how it must be, and you have to be a good boy and do what the ladies on the train tell you to do. You're not a baby anymore, but a big boy of seven.'"

To England

Kurt left Austria for the United Kingdom early in 1939. Families in Norwich, England, had volunteered to take in **refugee** children. Refugees are people who have been forced to leave their home, often because of war.

Kurt thought the journey was an adventure. He took a train to the coast. Then he and the other children got onto a boat. They crossed the sea at night. Nurses cared for the children and served them tea. In the morning, he was in a new country.

Many of the children arrived in England with nowhere to go. They lived in empty summer camps.

Reunion

Kurt Fuchel was lucky. His parents managed to escape from Austria and find their way to France. A French family hid them from the Nazis. Many other children's parents were killed during the war. These children grew up in the United Kingdom.

After the war, Kurt's parents stayed in France. In 1947 Kurt joined them there. He was 16 years old.

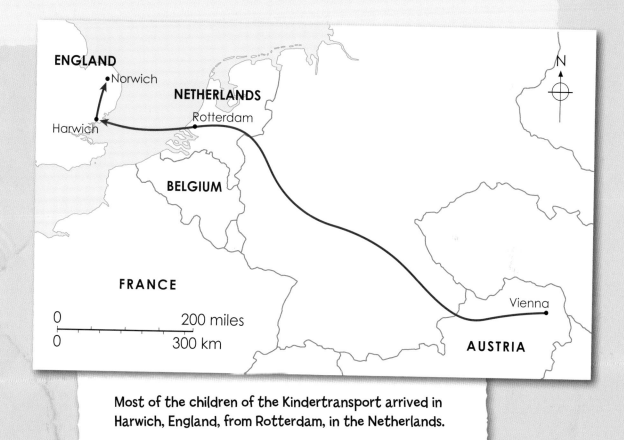

Most of the children of the Kindertransport arrived in Harwich, England, from Rotterdam, in the Netherlands.

HELPING HAND

The Association of Jewish Refugees helps the survivors of the Holocaust living in the United Kingdom, including many who escaped on the Kindertransport.

Russia: 2000

Aliyah is a **Hebrew** word. It refers to the immigration of Jewish people to Israel. Today, many Jews move to Israel because of anti-Semitism in other countries.

Alona moved more than 3,200 kilometers (2,000 miles) from Russia to Israel.

Alona Poupesheva

Alona Poupesheva grew up in Yekaterinburg, a city in central Russia. When she was six years old, she saw the word *Jew* on her mother's identity card. When she asked her about it, her mother said, "Don't worry about it, nobody at your school knows." It was Alona's first sense of anti-Semitism in Russia.

When Alona was 14, she wanted to change her life. She felt she had to move somewhere else if she wanted to succeed. Then she saw an advertisement for the Na'aleh High School Program in Israel. This is a program run by the Jewish Agency for Israel. It pays all expenses, or costs, for students who want to study in Israel. Alona applied and was accepted.

Today, many children immigrate to Israel from Russia, Africa, and the Middle East.

In Israel

Alona went to a school in Haifa. This city is in western Israel, on the Mediterranean Sea. She chose Haifa because it was the only city whose name she knew. It turned out to be a wonderful place to live. For the next three years she lived in a youth village. This is like a boarding school where immigrants in Israel live and study together.

Alona lived in a youth village like this one when she moved to Haifa.

DAILY LIFE

There are 50 youth villages across Israel. They are like boarding schools run by the government. More than 15,000 children and teenagers live and study there. Some are immigrants who traveled on their own. Others come from families who can no longer care for them.

After school

After high school, Alona joined the Israeli army. She served in the **canine** unit. This means she worked with dogs. She was awarded a medal after she and her dog stopped a truck carrying explosives. She may have saved many lives in her new country.

Today, Alona is studying political science in college. She wants to work in government.

HELPING HAND

Alona's parents taught her to be independent and supported her move to Israel. Today, she understands how strong they had to be to let her go.

Home at Last

On May 15, 1948, the modern state of Israel was **founded**. As part of its Declaration of Independence, the new nation opened its arms to immigration by Jewish people from around the world. The wandering was over. Finally, the Jewish people had a home.

Between 1948 and 1950, nearly half a million people immigrated to Israel. About half were refugees from European countries. Some were people who had been freed from Nazi concentration camps. Others had lost their homes during the war. Many of them were children.

The Jordan River runs through this valley. Many Jewish people consider it to be the border of their homeland.

New communities

Today, Jewish people continue to migrate. Many cities have communities of Jewish immigrants from Arab nations, such as Iran and Iraq. Since the 1980s, many Jews have fled the Eastern European countries that were once part of the **Soviet Union**. But these Jewish people are not wanderers. They have made new homes in new nations.

Jewish people have built new communities in cities around the world. These Jews are in Stamford Hill, London.

HELPING HAND
The Jewish Agency for Israel helps people who want to settle in Israel. They have special programs to help young immigrants who are living on their own. They also help poor children in Israel.

Mapping Migration

Arctic Ocean

Some of the children in this book traveled thousands of miles to find a place they could call home. Their experiences as children made them into the people they became as adults.

NORTH AMERICA

Milwaukee
Chicago

U.S.

Pacific Ocean

Atlantic Ocean

Golda Meir

Golda Meir traveled from Russia to Milwaukee, Wisconsin, in the United States. As an adult, she moved to Israel before it was even a country.

SOUTH AMERICA

Arctic Ocean

Kurt Fuchel

Kurt Fuchel traveled with the Kindertransport from Vienna to Norwich, in the United Kingdom. Later, he joined his family in France.

EUROPE

Yekaterinburg

ASIA

Norwich
London
Rotterdam
Gotha
Kiev
Vienna

Haifa

Alona Poupesheva

Alona Poupesheva left her home in Russia to find a new home in Israel.

AFRICA

Indian Ocean

Ralph Rehbock

Ralph Rehbock fled to the Netherlands and the United Kingdom before moving to Chicago. He was lucky to have relatives in the United States whom he could live with.

Glossary

aliyah Hebrew word that refers to the immigration of Jews to Israel

anti-Semitism prejudice against Jewish people. Many Jewish people have left their homes because of anti-Semitism.

canine referring to dogs. Dogs work with police officers in a "canine unit."

concentration camp prison for Jews and other prisoners of the Nazis during World War II. Many people were killed in concentration camps.

culture customs and beliefs that are shared by a group of people, including language, food, and music. Jewish people are joined by a common culture.

customs everyday activities and behaviors of people in an area. Immigrants often have to learn the customs of their new country.

found create or set up. The state of Israel was founded in 1948.

ghetto section of a city where one group of people is forced to live. During World War II, many Jews lived in ghettos.

government group of people that makes laws and rules by which a country is run

Hebrew traditional language of the Jewish people

Holocaust killing of Jews and other people by the Nazis during World War II. People who lived through the Holocaust are often called "survivors."

immigrant someone who comes in to live in another country

Kindertransport program that rescued thousands of Jewish children from Germany and nearby countries during World War II. The Kindertransport was run by the British government and other groups.

migrate/migration move/act of moving from one country to another

Nazi member of the National Socialist Party in Germany from the 1920s to 1940s. The Nazis considered Jewish people, gypsies, and some disabled people enemies of the state.

Palestine area of the Middle East at the east end of the Mediterranean Sea. Most of Palestine is now part of Israel.

pogrom organized violence against Jews in Russia. Most pogroms happened in the late 1800s and early 1900s.

prejudice belief that people are not good because of the way they look or because they are different in some way

refugee person forced to leave home to find safety outside his or her country, usually because of war or a natural disaster

Soviet Union country in Europe that broke up in 1991 to form many different countries, including Russia, Ukraine, and Lithuania

volunteer work by choice without pay

World War II war that took place from 1939 to 1945. In Europe the United Kingdom, Soviet Union, and other allies fought against Germany and Italy. An estimated six million Jews were killed in Nazi concentration camps during World War II.

Find Out More

Books

Davidson, Susanna. *Anne Frank*. Tulsa, Okla.: EDC, 2006.

Frank, Anne. *The Diary of a Young Girl*. New York: Alfred A. Knopf, 2010.

Marx, Trish, and Cindy Karp. *Sharing Our Homeland: Palestinian and Jewish Children at Summer Peace Camp*. New York: Lee & Low, 2010.

Zullo, Allan, and Mara Bovsun. *Survivors: True Stories of Children in the Holocaust*. New York: Scholastic, 2004.

DVD

Into the Arms of Strangers: Stories of the Kindertransport (2000)
An Oscar-winning documentary about the Kindertransport. This movie is best for older children.

Websites

www.annefrank.org
Learn about Anne Frank, a Jewish girl whose diary describing her experiences in hiding from the Nazis has become world famous.

www.uri.org/kids/world_juda.htm
Learn more about Judaism at this website.

Places to visit

United States Holocaust Memorial Museum
100 Raoul Wallenberg Place, SW
Washington, D.C. 20024-2126
Tel: (202) 488-0400
This museum features an extensive collection of documents, artifacts, and more that tell the story of the Holocaust. The exhibit "Remember the Children: Daniel's Story" is designed specifically for kids.

Illinois Holocaust Museum and Education Center
9603 Woods Drive
Skokie, Illinois 60077
Tel: (847) 967-4800
This museum focuses on the Holocaust, the stories of survivors, and the lessons that can be learned from the Holocaust.

Index